ICE AGE MEGA BEASTS

MONSTER BIRDS

by Sara Gilbert

CREATIVE EDUCATION • CREATIVE PAPERBACKS

364.2743

Published by Creative Education and Creative Paperbacks
P.O. Box 227, Mankato, Minnesota 56002
Creative Education and Creative Paperbacks are
imprints of **The Creative Company**
www.thecreativecompany.us

Design and production by **Chelsey Luther**
Art direction by **Rita Marshall**
Printed in the **United States of America**

Photographs by Alamy (Stocktrek Images, Inc.), Corbis (Scientifica),
Dreamstime (Artesiawells, Tranac), FreeVectorMaps.com, Look and Learn
(Angus McBride), Newscom (Album/Florilegius), Science Source (Jaime
Chirinos, Tom McHugh, Walter Myers), Shutterstock (AKorolchuk), SuperStock
(DeAgostini/DeAgostini)

Library of Congress Cataloging-in-Publication Data
Gilbert, Sara.
Monster birds / Sara Gilbert.
p. cm. — (Ice age mega beasts)
Includes bibliographical references and index.
Summary: An elementary exploration of monster birds, focusing on fossil
evidence that helps explain how their wide wings and long feathers helped
these beasts adapt to the last Ice Age.

ISBN 978-1-60818-768-3 (hardcover)
ISBN 978-1-62832-376-4 (pbk)
ISBN 978-1-56660-810-7 (eBook)
1. Extinct birds—Juvenile literature. 2. Birds—Juvenile literature.

QL676.8 G54 2017
598.168—dc23   2016014628

CCSS: RI.1.1, 2, 3, 4, 5, 6, 7, 10; RI.2.1, 2, 4, 5, 6, 7, 10; RI.3.1, 2, 4, 5, 7, 10;
RF.1.1, 2, 3, 4; RF.2.3, 4; RF.3.3, 4

First Edition HC 9 8 7 6 5 4 3 2 1
First Edition PBK 9 8 7 6 5 4 3 2 1

Contents

The Wonder Bird

The sky is bright blue. The sun is shining. But a large shadow moves across the sky. It's not a cloud. It's a teratorn!

Teratorns were the largest of the many monster birds of the Ice Age.

The word "teratorn" means "wonder bird." Teratorns may have been the biggest flying birds ever. Their wings spread almost 24 feet (7.3 m) across!

Today, the bird with the longest wingspan is the wandering albatross, at 10 feet (3 m).

Ice Age Hunters

Birds were the only relatives of dinosaurs left during the last Ice Age. There were several giant birds that flew above huge sheets of ice called glaciers.

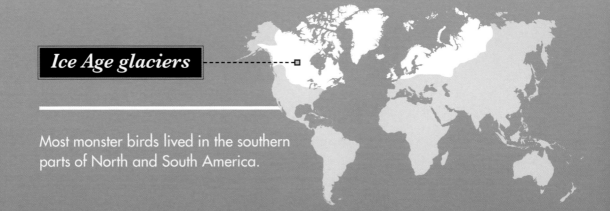

Ice Age glaciers

Most monster birds lived in the southern parts of North and South America.

These monster birds were fierce *predators*. Some, like teratorns, hunted fish. Other giant birds ate *mammals* that had died, too.

Teratorns likely swallowed fish and other small animals whole.

Open Spaces

Teratorns and other big birds lived in open spaces. Their wings were too wide to fly in thick forests. They soared over large areas looking for food.

Monster birds fearlessly chased saber-toothed cats away from food.

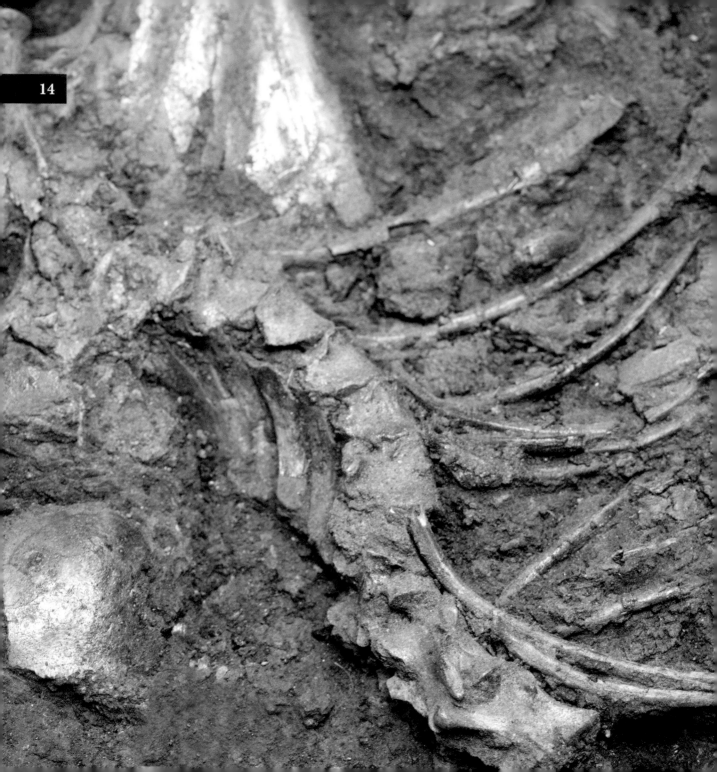

Fossils of the biggest teratorns ever were found in Argentina. Hundreds of other fossils came from a tar pit in California. The birds got stuck there long ago and died.

La Brea Tar Pits

The first teratorn fossil was found in California's La Brea Tar Pits in 1909.

Argentina

Monstrous Size

The biggest teratorns were as tall as a person. They could weigh almost 200 pounds (90.7 kg). A single feather could be 59 inches (150 cm) long.

elephant calf = **200 pounds**

A big monster bird had to run downhill to be able to fly from a spot on the ground.

Most teratorns were smaller. They weighed 30 pounds (13.6 kg) or less. They had short legs and wide bodies. They slowly stalked their *prey* on the ground.

Teratorns were about the weight of Andean condors, which weigh up to 33 pounds (15 kg).

Earth warmed when the Ice Age ended. The landscape changed as glaciers melted. Some kinds of prey became harder to find. Eight thousand years ago, the monster birds died out.

Many Ice Age animals died in California's tar pits, where their bones were kept safe.

Teratorn Close-up

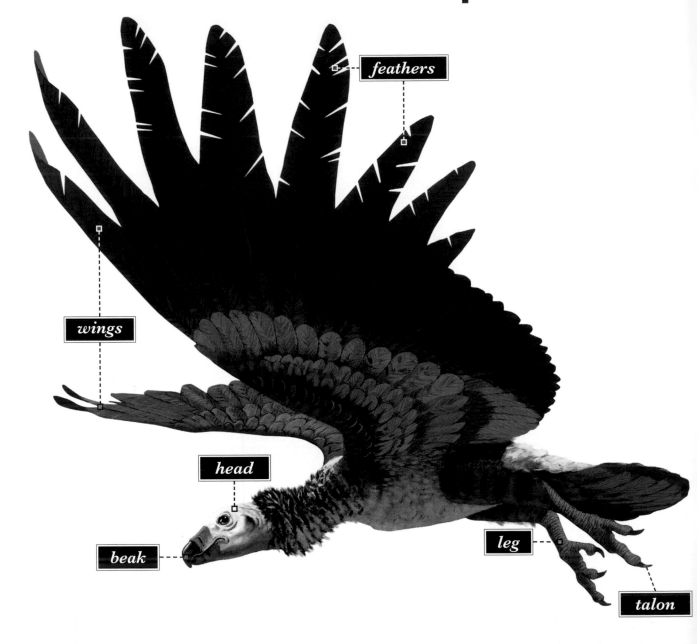

feathers

wings

head

beak

leg

talon

Glossary

fossils: remains of animals or plants

mammals: warm-blooded animals with fur or hair who feed their young milk

predators: animals that hunt other animals for food

prey: animals that are hunted and eaten by other animals

Read More

Lindsay, William. *Eyewitness Prehistoric Life.* New York: DK, 2012.

Turner, Alan. *National Geographic Prehistoric Mammals.* Washington, D.C.: National Geographic, 2004.

Websites

Enchanted Learning: Ice Age Mammals
http://www.enchantedlearning.com/subjects /mammals/Iceagemammals.shtml
Learn more about the Ice Age and the animals that lived then.

KidzSearch: Teratorn
http://www.kidzsearch.com/wiki/Teratorn
Find facts about teratorns.

Note: Every effort has been made to ensure that the websites listed above are suitable for children, that they have educational value, and that they contain no inappropriate material. However, because of the nature of the Internet, it is impossible to guarantee that these sites will remain active indefinitely or that their contents will not be altered.

Index